*With love
from*

_____

to

_____

LITTLE ☆ STARS™

SAGITTARIUS

A parent's guide to the little star of the family

JOHN ASTROP

with illustrations by the author

ELEMENT

Shaftesbury, Dorset ● Rockport, Massachusetts
Brisbane, Queensland

© John Astrop 1994

Published in Great Britain in 1994 by
Element Books Ltd.
Longmead, Shaftesbury, Dorset

Published in the USA in 1994 by
Element, Inc.
42 Broadway, Rockport, MA 01966

Published in Australia in 1994 by
Element Books Ltd.
for Jacaranda Wiley Ltd.
33 Park Road, Milton, Brisbane, 4064

Printed and bound in Great Britain by
BPC Paulton Books Ltd.

British Library Cataloguing in Publication
data available

Library of Congress Cataloguing in publication
data available

ISBN 1-85230-545-2

CONTENTS

THE TWELVE SIGNS

Everyone knows a little about the twelve sun signs. It's the easiest way to approach real astrology without going to the trouble of casting up a chart for the exact time of birth. You won't learn everything about a person with the sun sign but you'll know a lot more than if you just use observation and guesswork. The sun is in roughly the same sign and degree of the zodiac at the same time every year. It's a nice astronomical event that doesn't need calculating. So if you're born between

May 22 and June 21 you'll be pretty sure you're a Gemini; between June 22 and July 23 then you're a Cancer and so on. Many people say how can you divide the human race into twelve sections and are there only twelve different types. Well for a start most people make assessments and judgements on their fellow humans with far smaller groups than that. Rich and poor, educated and non-educated, town girl, country boy, etc. Even with these very simple pigeon holes we can combine to make 'Rich educated town boy' and 'poor non-educated country girl'. We try to get as much information as we can about the others that we make relationships with through life. Astrology as a way of describing and understanding others is unsurpassed. Take the traditional meaning of the twelve signs:

Aries - is self-assertive, brave, energetic and pioneering.

Taurus - is careful, possessive, values material things, is able to build and make things grow.

Gemini - is bright-minded, curious, communicative and versatile.

Cancer - is sensitive, family orientated, protective and caring.

Leo - is creative, dramatic, a leader, showy and generous.

Virgo - is organised, critical, perfectionist and practical.

Libra - is balanced, diplomatic, harmonious, sociable, and likes beautiful things.

Scorpio - is strong-willed, magnetic, powerful, extreme, determined and recuperative.

Sagittarius - is adventurous, philosophical, far-thinking, blunt, truth-seeking.

Capricorn - is cautious, responsible, patient, persistent and ambitious.

Aquarius - is rebellious, unorthodox, humanitarian, idealistic, a fighter of good causes.

Pisces - is sensitive, imaginative, caring, visionary and sacrificing.

If you can find anyone in your circle of friends and acquaintances who isn't described pretty neatly by one of the above it would be surprising. Put the twelve signs into different lives and occupations and you see how it works. A Taurean priest would be more likely to devote his life to looking after the physical and material needs of his church members, feeding the poor, setting up charities. A Virgoan bank robber would plan meticulously and never commit spontaneous crimes. A Leo teacher would make learning an entertainment and a pleasure for her pupils.

So with parents and children. A Capricorn child handles the business of growing up and learning in a very different way to a Libran child. A Scorpio parent manages the family quite differently to an Aquarian. The old boast, 'I'm very fair, I treat all my children the same', may not be the best way to help your little ones at all. Our individual drive is the key to making a success of life. The time when we need the most acceptance of the way we are is in childhood. As a parent it's good to know the ways in which our little ones are like us but we must never forget the ways in which they are different.

LITTLE SAGITTARIUS

For the next few years you are privileged to nurture the fireball energy and adventurous spirit of a wild little mare or stallion. Horses have traditionally been associated with this sign, the Centaur with the bow and arrow aimed high in the air, just on the point of galloping into the middle distance. Your little star is a natural born adventurer, outgoing, exuberant, and driven by sheer enthusiasm to travel further than all the other signs of the zodiac. Mentally and physically that is, and if they're not disappearing round the end of the road, adventure bound, they're asking questions, questions, questions! The planet that rules Sagittarius is Jupiter and this, being the benefic or expansively lucky planet, does its job well with these friendly little characters. They arrive anywhere at any time, beaming and full of good humour, expecting to be well received by all and sundry, and are rarely disappointed in this assumption. It will not be long before you realise that there is nothing devious or hid-

den in the little Archer. Honest and straightforward in all that they do or say, they'd turn purple with green stripes if they told a lie. At least if they tried they would be so inept as to make it ridiculously unbelievable. Their whole being seeks the truth and all their experience pushes them further and

further to find out just what this old world is really all about. From now on, nothing you say will be taken for granted. Not that you won't be trusted but there will be a genuine desire to know how you came to your conclusions. The whys, hows and whens will rain on you till you fall exhausted at the end of the day. Tired and bemused, you'll fall prey to the bubbling friendliness the very next morning and be back again with the answers. It's around this time that you'll start to fill the home with travel books and encyclopedias scattered casually on every side table and bookshelf. Phew! The high-spirited little Sagittarian's honesty makes for plenty of hilarious faux pas. Always expecting to get a straight answer, they dish out the same treatment to others, but with the best will in the world, these are the champions at opening their mouths and putting their foot in it! The long chain of affronted aunts, humiliated second cousins, and offended friends will be on your conscience continually. It's not just childish unawareness either for your little Sagittarian will tell it like it is on every occasion for the rest of his good-natured, blundering life. You may have to settle for 'you look really good Mom, for someone as old as you!' as a compliment; it was meant as one!

When it comes to learning, they consume it by the bucketful; when it comes to play, they throw in their heart and soul. Who's going to worry about a little mistiming or a few blunt words when you have a friend like this?

The Baby

Cuddlesome as they are, these little rascals wriggle when you hold them as if they had an urgent appointment somewhere else. This tiny traveller will kick around all day in the cot too, almost as if he can't wait to get this baby business over, get on his feet and up, up and away! Changing pants and cleaning-up operations can become

a little like trying to put a diaper on a set of bagpipes. The theme of freedom at all costs, even as early as this, sets the scenario for the rest of the bold little Sagittarian's life. As soon as this one is put down on the ground there will be a brave attempt at clawing, kicking and a neat little side flip that gets the body moving toward the goal, which is usually at the far side of the room.

Two days' practice and you'll be surprised how difficult it is to keep your little Archer in the same room as you. Once you realise that this one means to travel, out comes the biggest affront to any Sagittarian, the play pen! Does he settle down like a good little babe and play with his toes? No he doesn't! And if you can take the heart-rending sight of your little bandido holding on to the bars of his prison with such a pitiful look in his eyes, well........

THE FIRST THREE YEARS

As a toddler, the smile really begins to become a permanent feature of your little star. Made for movement, she probably had been trying to get up on her feet almost as soon as she could crawl; now the games really start. You'll have a problem keeping up with the frenzy of activity that mobility inspires in little Sagittarius. Great little performers, they'll go over the top with reckless abandon, just to get your applause and admiration. Each new talent acquired sets your little adventurer onward looking for the next one at such a rate it could take your breath away. Speech comes quickly and as soon as a sentence can be put together you can bet it'll be a question! Running around is one way of finding out things and asking questions is the other. Little Sagittarius has the whole thing sorted out in no time at all and from then on you'll be run off your feet and talked speechless. It's never a chore though, tiring as it may be, for this bright little spark is the best company in the zodiac. Full of fun and always ready for a good session of fooling around, it may sometimes be a problem getting your little clown to take matters like feeding himself or potty training seriously. Be patient, for when the joke's over your little comedian will sort out the serious bits on his  own just as soon as it becomes more convenient for his busy life if he can master them. If you haven't made sure that the day's ration of powerhouse energy is all used up before bedtime, you'll get three or four visits during your evening's TV viewing, for snacks and more adventure stories, until the last little glow fizzles out. Please don't wake us too early in the morning!

THE KINDERGARTEN

The creative atmosphere and the host of potential pals makes nursery school a dream come true and for the first few days your little Sagittarian will be in a haze of activity and rushing around. When the excitement settles you will be surprised how well your small Archer gets on with the rest of the children. Always popular, the little Sagittarian is never backward in coming forward and will take a leading role in initiating most of the good-natured horseplay in the class. For this reason there will be little mishaps as your youngster

cannot resist going just a bit further than everyone else. Trying to jump higher, run faster, and climb higher will result in a few grazed knees and bruised elbows, but that is the price the adventurer pays.

SCHOOL AND ONWARDS

Little Sagittarians want to learn; they've spent long enough trying to prise all the available information they can out of you and now the prospect of actually being in a place where they make you do it is heaven! Quick to learn and popular in the class, a great combination for what may be the happiest years of a little Sagittarian's life, if you don't count the rest. All this will go smoothly in the early years, when Junior will enter into each new project with great gusto, becoming a vital and leading member of the class. Over the years, when the novelty fades a

little there may be a slacking off of interest in certain areas that haven't managed to keep their excitement. Even homework gets neglected later on in favour of a very necessary visit to a friend round the corner. All in all though, when the big exams arrive Sagittarius will pull a few rabbits out of the hat, a little bit bigger and better than you'd expected. As little Sagittarius grows up the sense of adventure takes her further afield more and more often and you'll begin using the old cliché 'You treat this home like an hotel!' Take a tip, if you want to catch up on the Archer's latest news, don't offer room service!

THE THREE DIFFERENT
TYPES OF SAGITTARIUS

THE DECANATES

Astrology traditionally divides each of the signs into three equal parts of ten degrees called the decanates. These give a slightly different quality to the sign depending on whether the child is born in the first, second or third ten days of the thirty-day period when one is in a sign. Each third is ruled by one of the three signs in the same element. Sagittarius is a Fire sign and the three Fire signs are Sagittarius, Aries and Leo. The nature of Fire signs is basically creative so the following three types each has a different way of expressing their creative abilities.

First Decanate - Nov. 23 to Dec. 2

This is the part of Sagittarius that is most typical of the sign qualities. Sagittarius is an adventurer. The eternal search for this sign is truth and each will look for this in their own way. Not being able to bear to do anything half-heartedly they must seek to push to the furthest possibilities in whatever occupation they choose. Writers delve deeper into human character and themselves to find reality, musicians explore uncharted territory and find new modes of expression. Jupiterian Sagittarians travel hopefully both physically and mentally all their lives. Their slips of the tongue let skeletons out of closets, knock the wind out of the sails of pomposity and cut across hypocrisy and half-truths. They are not always loved for it, but they are usually forgiven and they are nearly always funny. It is told that when a reprimanding lady said to Sagittarian Winston Churchill, 'Sir, you are disgustingly drunk!', the old statesman swayed a little, slowly lit up his longest of all cigars and replied, 'and you Madame are very ugly, but in the morning I'll be sober!' Look at the list, from Jonathan Swift to Bette Midler they're all exponents of the blunt and painful put-down. Harpo Marx managed to do it without saying a word!

Second Decanate - Dec. 3 to Dec. 12

This is the Self-willed Adventurer. Sharing some of the qualities of Aries and Mars with Sagittarius, these characters are the most powerful combination of the three. Enormous energy, loads of creative talent and the power to keep going beyond most normal people's abilities. Great performers, their intense enthusiasm can carry an audience or a devoted following with ease. These Sagittarians are much more loners than the other two, needing little help or cooperation in order to function well. They take more risks on all levels and push to greater limits. It's not so strange that two of the hell-raising showbiz gang, Sammy Davis Junior and Frank Sinatra, were both born in this daredevil decanate. Sinatra did it his way, but sadly Jim Morrison's reckless way went a little too far, too soon. Bhagwan Shree Rajneesh put together his own Sagittarian truth, a mixture of Eastern philosophy and Western group therapy, and carried thousands of red-clothed devotees (red is the Mars colour), wearing little portraits of their leader, on to who knows where.

Third Decanate - Dec. 13 to Dec. 21
This is the Creative Adventurer and is where the mixture gets a little royal blood with a

combination of the qualities of Leo and Sagittarius. Whatever has been said about the other Sagittarians, this decanate adds large scale and a personality that takes for granted their regal position. Famous characters from this part of the sign show, in either their own bearing or in their large-scale work, a presence that makes them big establishment figures. Beethoven's grand and powerful symphonies, for instance, and the suave Noel Coward, king of the theatre on both sides of the Atlantic for a long and happy reign. The biggest box office adventure films of the century have come from the direction of Steven Spielberg, and if Indiana Jones isn't the all-time Sagittarian hero personified I'll eat his hat. When Sagittarians travel they really travel far, with both Spielberg and Arthur C. Clarke exploring other worlds in their imaginative fantasies. Tiny Edith Piaf, the French 'sparrow', dominated the stage as queen of the dramatic ballad and in true Sagittarian fashion 'regretted nothing'.

OTHER LITTLE SAGITTARIANS

Mums and Dads like you delighted in bringing up the following little adventurers. Yours will probably turn out to be even more famous!

First Decanate Sagittarius

Giovanni Bellini, Jonathan Swift, William Blake, Toulouse Lautrec, Billy the Kid, Sir Winston Churchill, Mark Twain, Manuel de Falla, Boris Karloff, Sir John Barbirolli, Bruce Lee, Dorothy Lamour, Jimi Hendrix, Randy Newman, Tina Turner, Harpo Marx, Bette Midler.

Second Decanate Sagittarius

Mary Queen of Scots, Joseph Conrad, Christina Rossetti, Diego Rivera, Walt Disney, Bagwan Shree Rajneesh, Frank Sinatra, Sammy Davis Junior, James Thurber, Louis Prima, Jim Morrison, Dionne Warwick, Dave Brubeck, Tom Waits, Kim Basinger, Jeff Bridges.

Third Decanate Sagittarius

Jane Austen, Gustave Flaubert, Ludwig van Beethoven, Paul Klee, Noel Coward, Edith Piaf, J. Paul Getty, Willi Brandt, Dr Margaret Mead, Steven Spielberg, Arthur C. Clarke, Betty Grable, Don Johnson, Jane Fonda, Uri Geller, Keifer Sutherland, Jeff Chandler.

AND NOW THE
PARENTS

THE ARIES PARENT

The good news!

The two of you are in for a good old fiery enthusiastic barrel of fun. Both share a love of activity, adventure, and the outdoors. Aries encourages with enthusiasm the expression of little Sagittarius's natural free-ranging individual approach to life. Although always active and on the move, this little one is a thinker and has to understand the truth of everything in order to develop fully. Straight answers, even if they hurt a little, are the basis and the strength of this relationship.

Aries is a natural authority figure and providing there is always reason and logic behind limitations to this child's freedom the little Archer will cooperate gracefully. Both need challenges, but Sagittarius's vision is long-distance and without Aries's help

may miss immediate opportunities while looking towards tomorrow. Plenty of rough and tumble play helps this relationship keep healthy and close but do remember that you're both more than a little accident prone and bumped heads and grazed knees could be the order of the day when you encourage each other to extremes. The apparent toughness of this child (even the little Sagittarian girls are often tomboys) can give Aries the mistaken notion that learning life's lessons the hard way is best for little Sagittarius. They may well deal bravely with being thrown in at the deep end but not unless they get plenty of affection and warm love as well. Love of animals usually features strongly in the lives of these little adventurers and, bearing in mind the Sagittarian need for the great outdoors, a pup would be a great asset. The Archer has a sharp brain and a creative approach that will delight and often surprise the Aries parent with its maturity. When this little bowman shoots an arrow in the air it usually arrives well on target. Get little Sagittarius to share ideas with you to develop confidence.

...and now the bad news!

The biggest clash for you two fiery characters can come from Aries overreacting and losing patience with Sagittarius's continual 'why?' to every order. Your little one wants the truth and no bullying bluster will take the place of a good logical answer. The answer 'Because I said so' will never get results, and this normally easy-going child can become a permanent opponent, or look for logic elsewhere. All cards between the two of you should be played face up on the table. Some of little Sagittarius's may turn out to be a little blunt but at least you'll stay good pals.

THE TAURUS PARENT

The good news!

You like a light, bright and pleasant home that runs like clockwork for the comfort and pleasure of everyone in the family. The Sagittarian child is happy-go-lucky, freedom-loving and wields disarming honesty like a blunt instrument. The Taurean parent's well-organised set of rules to keep the family on an even keel will get little respect or obedience until all the 'whys' and 'hows' are convincingly answered. Junior's natural curiosity craves and accumulates knowledge, but never without question. Taurean patience can work wonders with this delightful little intellectual adventurer, but later a couple of dozen good reference books may provide extra support. Often blissfully unaware of clumsiness with word and action, Junior's 'Sorry I trod on your toe, but you've got such huge feet, Mum' will have to be endured until you've successfully explained why the obvious truth is sometimes unacceptable. This couple share a love of Mother Nature, though Taurus may prefer pottering about the garden to Sagittarius's

impulse to aim for the far-distant horizon. In fact the great difference between you is that whereas Taureans love the home comforts, little Sagittarians, once they get sufficiently independent, only see home as a base for a quick snack and a sleep between adventures. With the amount of time and trouble that you take putting together the very best of cosy abodes you may sometimes wonder if it is all worthwhile. Yes it is! Like the travellers of old they'll bring back tales of their exploits that'll delight and amuse you for years to come.

...and now the bad news!

This love of freedom can make for extra itchy feet if Taurus becomes overpossessive and restrictive. Even sitting in the same room with you, little Sagittarians can be a million miles away if you put them under pressure. Don't forget that they travel mentally as well as physically. You'll just have to accept that this little one needs your support but will not want to stick around the home when he's got it. Trust produces a more positive result and an adoring little Archer that will always return to rest weary limbs with dear ol' Mom and Dad at the end of an exhausting adventure will repay the concession.

THE GEMINI PARENT

The good news!

The enthusiastic quest for knowledge and experience is shared by this perpetual-motion duo. The rest of the household may find the pace and action of this high-spirited youngster and 'Peter Pan' parent a trial, but this couple will love it. Sagittarians need freedom and the open road and even Gemini can be amazed at how quickly, after learning to crawl, this little Archer can reach supersonic speeds. A door left ajar sees Junior disappearing down the corridor in seconds. This adventurous dash sums up the young Sagittarian's approach to learning and Gemini will find a close affinity to such an optimistic child. This parent's talent for invention will easily provide plenty of shared projects to develop confidence and understanding in the young Sagittarian. The little Archer's love of truth demands and respects straight answers to all questions and gives the same in return. Such honesty may often cause alarm in its blunt, unabashed

frankness and some gentle but reasonable guidance may be necessary to avoid Junior continually opening his mouth and putting his foot in it. Sagittarius's knack of saying the wrong thing at the wrong time is renowned and comes usually out of years of practice on stunned victims. Step in early Gemini; with your wit you should be able to help produce at least one moderately tactful Sagittarian. In the end it won't matter greatly as their genuine, well-meaning, love of life shines through and all is forgiven!

...and now the bad news!

Although you have masses in common, especially a driving curiosity concerning anything and everything in life, there can be a couple of difficulties in this otherwise sparkling relationship. The Gemini mind works on a sharp, quickly changing level that drops a subject or activity as soon as enough has been extracted from it for all useful purposes. This doesn't suit Sagittarius's need to stay with a subject until the deepest parts of it have been explored. Your different ways of seeing things will from time to time produce clashes of ideas but nothing so serious that a well-suited couple like you won't be able to talk out sensibly. Remember that Sagittarians are long-distance travellers and that means in the mind as well, so leave your small adventurer to finish one journey before starting the next.

THE CANCER PARENT

The good news!

The Cancer parent is imaginative, understanding, and will feel intuitively the Sagittarian's need to be free to try out things for himself. It may be disconcerting at first to find Junior fighting shy of material hugs and disappearing into the middle distance on supermarket trips, but that's the adventurous Archer. With this child's need to understand the truth of anything, the Cancer parent would be well advised not lay down rules and regulations without first explaining why, in good logical terms. And the reasons had better be selfless, for Sagittarius can detect dishonesty quickly with a couple of well-aimed questions and the blunt frankness of the answer will set you back on your heels. Although Junior will probably find out sooner than most that Father Christmas is only Dad tripping over the train-set, this is no down-to-earth, dreary realist. Cancer and Sagittarius will share impossible dreams, romantic adventures and hilarious revels (usually as a result of one of Sagittarius's naively frank 'faux pas'). Fortunately for this relationship the Crab's sense of humour runs high and almost all sticky situations will be laughed out of existence. You will constantly be proud of this little character's exploits and sheer

boldness in taking on the big old world outside and may have to bite your lip in order to stop yourself stepping between your little wonderchild and danger every second of the long day. Cancerians, because you are the most caring of parents, are the greatest worriers. There are more than a few Cancerian Grannies still worrying about their fifty-year-old Sagittarian daughters. Little or big Sagittarians learn by getting out there and trying things out for themselves. You'll have to allow for a few bruises.

...and now the bad news!

Cancers usually go for the sidestep where family troubles are concerned, but from time to time their own basic protective nature gets the better of them and produces the very problems that they wish to avoid. Yes, the old worryguts problem rears its head again. Troubles escalate if Cancer's protectiveness and need to be close requires constant reassurance from Sagittarius about elusive behaviour. Love and independence go together for the Archer, but love with strings just brings on claustrophobia. Sagittarians are to be shared and lucky old us to have plenty around.

♌

THE LEO PARENT

The good news!

This is a very agreeable blend of signs, and parent and child should have no trouble in striking up a relaxed, harmonious relationship. The happy-go-lucky Sagittarius child will find an appreciative audience in the Leo parent. Good-humoured Leo will revel in the young Archer's sense of fun, joining in with the horseplay, laughing at the jokes and soon becoming a good friend rather than just a parent. When Junior pops out for 'five minutes' and doesn't turn up till three hours later, Leo Mom or Dad won't resist a smile when giving a cursory dressing down, understanding fully the little Sagittarian's wanderlust. These free-ranging youngsters often give their parents red faces by coming out with blunt comments in public; the saying that 'many a truth is spoken from the mouth of a child' was surely coined with such 'Honest Johns' in mind. Although this is normally good

entertainment to fun-loving Leo, the Lion's phenomenal pride may occasionally suffer a blow through an ill-timed Sagittarian faux pas. The Leo Mom or Dad can encourage this youngster's sense of humour but provide a few guidelines, pointing out that sometimes the truth hurts and that, quite simply, some people can't take a joke if it's a little too near the truth for comfort. You'll never quite stop little Sagittarius dropping the occasional bricks but at least you can try to prevent them falling on other people's toes. Discipline should present no problems provided the Leo parent uses reason rather than dogmatic 'bossiness'. Fair play gets this little one's respect.

...and now the bad news!

The desire to see their progeny successful and achieving well can sometimes lead Leos into pushing their children into ventures unprepared.

Sagittarians are quick on the uptake but are individualists and like to do things at their own pace and in their own way. The resulting clash of wills can be extreme, with a lot of over-the-top dramatics leading to the small Archer making off for the wide open spaces or a sulk in the backyard. You're a powerhouse of a team working on the same side so as long as you just coach from the sidelines you'll have plenty to be a proud old lion about.

THE VIRGO PARENT

The good news!

The best part of your relationship will be the talk. Both of you have plenty to say, with little Sagittarius seeing life as a great quest for knowledge and you a fund of good information, facts and figures. You like a quiet and smooth-running life but you ain't gonna get it with this little darling! Great fun it may be, but you'll have both hands constantly full looking after this lively little enthusiast. Small Sagittarians have bags of fun-loving energy and a spirit of adventure that keeps them constantly on the move. In no way clinging vines, these little wanderers need a long, long, rein or if they had a say in the matter, none at all. Even the explorer needs a home base and the Virgoan's good organisation and well proven systems provide a more than adequate support for little Sagittarius's free-ranging exploits. Your Virgo attention to detail and down-to-earth practicality can equip this little one with a good grounding in common sense. This commodity the Virgoan parent may equate with intelligence, but this youngster, whilst sometimes lacking the former, has more than a fair share of

the latter. The search for truth is Sagittarius's basic drive and if throwing a little caution to the wind gets the desired result, then so be it. The best way to get through to Junior is straight talk and good logic handed out as friend to friend, and you'll receive the same honest treatment in return. Being modest yourself you may need to understand that Archers, like the other Fire signs, need a regular dose of admiration and encouragement for their efforts and will wilt and quickly lose interest in projects that you set up if they don't get them. They won't get big headed, just recharged with even more energy! Whew!

...and now the bad news!

You do like things to be done properly and... Sagittarians are impulsive and spontaneous, two qualities that guarantee that things won't necessarily be done properly or even well. Just like the song immortalised by Sagittarian Frank Sinatra, 'I did it my way', so it is with your little Archer. Nagging and nit-picking will only guarantee a clean pair of heels moving quickly into the middle distance, mentally if not physically. Keep it friendly and fun and the wanderer will return. Get into partnership with outdoor sports and games, shopping expeditions, exploring countryside and town, and plenty of travel and information books for quieter moments – if there ever are any!

♎

THE LIBRA PARENT

The good news!

The companionable and caring Libran parent will delight in this little fun-loving, energetic adventurer. Life for the little Sagittarian is a series of doors to be opened and roads to be explored both physically and mentally. The close friendly attitude of the Libran will bring out the best of this youngster's natural honesty and warm affection. Keep it close but never cloying and possessive for Junior likes freedom above all things. Lots of talk and good healthy argument will keep the relationship busy, on the move, and a positive help in little Sagittarius's development of self-reliance. Neither parent nor child is excessively ambitious so pressure in these areas will be minimal. Little Sagittarius doesn't learn in order to compete, but purely to find out the truth. The Archer lays all the cards on the table and expects everyone else to. Straight answers to frank questions and this little one's happy. This blunt honesty, though always well meant, may get some adverse reactions from

the outside world if not aided with a large helping of the Libran's diplomacy. Getting over the point that other people are not always so fond of hearing the truth, especially if it hurts their feelings, is a gargantuan task for the

parents of this little one. There is little chance of serious clashes with this duo, as the combination of Libra's easy-going nature and Sagittarius's ability to see the funny side of everything makes flare-ups short, sharp and minimal. Just for fun you may have to stop being a lazy old luxury-loving Libra for a few years and join little Sagittarius in her love of outdoor fun and games, sport both played and watched. Above all, don't forget if it's at all possible a pet of some kind. The Sagittarian idea of perfection is a life full of adventure with a good lolloping mongrel to romp with. Sagittarians are traditionally the animal lovers supreme!

...and now the bad news!

It's almost impossible for you two to really get into battles, you just like each other too much. So where's the bad news? Nothing too serious but... You're an old softie with such a desire to please and keep everything happy where your loved ones are concerned that you can easily fall into the trap of constantly giving in to your little one's every whim. Yes, you spoil 'em! This is OK by them but not so good for those that have to pick up the pieces. Wives who take over after a doting, self-effacing Libran Mom has spoiled her new husband will not thank you for this lazy hulk. Next time you give in, remember, you'll not be losing a son, you'll be gaining a battling daughter-in-law!

THE SCORPIO PARENT

The good news!

For a Scorpio like you there is nothing more desirable than a good challenge – something that needs all the energy and drive of which you are eminently capable. This babe is it! The free-ranging, fun-loving Sagittarian child, more than a handful for any old everyday common or garden normal parent, will find your calm, cool and capable self a rock of support and a solid home base from which to plan all the adventurous exploits in the world. This understanding parent will admire

and encourage Junior's early self-confident wander-
ings in search of adventure, knowledge and above
all truth. Taking little at face value this youngster
must know why, where, and how, and if it doesn't
make sense, forget it. To this end nothing is sa-
cred to the blunt questions of the little Archer. This
honest approach will sometimes appear exasper-
atingly thoughtless and naive to the ever aware
Scorpio but the task of smoothing a few of the
rough edges will be
irresistible. The pow-
erful Scorpio, who
sometimes finds it dif-
ficult to resist 'You'll
do it because I said
so!' and is met with
Junior's 'Is that be-
cause you're bigger
than me?', may feel
more than a twinge of

guilt. No hurt intended, the little Archer really just wanted to know! With patient discussion, and a few more crushed egos later, Scorpio can help young Sagittarius resist dispensing freely the more devastating 'home truths'. The startling knowledge that others sometimes have to bend the facts a little to keep their dignity will, when proved, make for easier Sagittarian public relations. All this aside, Junior's one of the most entertaining fun-loving characters in the book and Scorpio the greatest enthusiast – not a bad combination for friends.

...and now the bad news!

The biggest clashes with this passionate couple will be over Sagittarius fighting for every kind of freedom and Scorpio restricting them. Protective as are all the water signs, little Sagittarius's need to be 'up, up and away' at every opportunity will drive Scorpio to imposing limitations on how late Junior can stay out, how far he can go, who can he go with, etc. This is usually more acute if the couple are opposite sexes. Moms with sons and Dads with daughters. A difficult balance to strike between safety and self-reliance. There's a challenge, Scorpio!!

THE SAGITTARIUS PARENT

The good news!

You could be the closest pals in the book. Both parent and child are intuitive, creative, exuberant and continuously on the move. As long as you are both travelling in the same direction this relationship has all the potential for a long-lasting, fun-loving, energetic friendship. There'll be no subterfuge, humbug or even 'white lies' with these two. Little Sagittarius will get all the answers straight from the shoulder and be expected to respond likewise. The search for truth dominates both big and little Sagittarians, and Junior's life quest for more and more knowledge will be well supported here. Developing early self-confidence, the little Archer soon gets itchy feet for the outside world. Quickly taking to kindergarten, school and visits anywhere, this little wanderer has no need to cling to the confines of home. The love of the great outdoors and adventure will see parent and child energetically sharing much physical activity (if you're rich enough, horses and large dogs are often invited to join in). The Sagittarian love of animals is renowned: maybe it's about the Archer being a

Centaur, half-man half-horse, anyway there's a special affinity which usually insists that there are a couple of pets on the agenda in any Sagittarian home. You also share a desire to get up and go to far away places and need to find out about other people in distant parts of the world and explore different ways of life. It's as if your little corner of the world is just not big enough to hold your big-thinking plans. Make sure that your junior partner gets a good grounding in how to read travel brochures and timetables.

...and now the bad news!

The problems with two Sagittarians is almost never about battles between the two of them but more the embarrassment that they create for the weaker souls around. Though ideal company for each other, Junior may never discover, in this straight honest relationship, that other people do not behave in the same open manner. This vital piece of information will take some learning as the Sagittarian art of wielding truth like a blunt instrument is compulsive. A trail of crushed egos does not make friends and influence people. Fortunately you guys usually come with a big heart and mostly you're forgiven in time for the next faux pas!

THE CAPRICORN PARENT

The good news!

No airy fairy qualities about the Capricorn parent. You are a realist, respect authority and have a fair and reasonable attitude to dishing it out yourself whilst conscientiously attending to the material needs of the family. In fact, the traditional firm but fair parent. Little Sagittarians are extrovert, fun-loving expenders of unlimited energy in every direction at once. The traditional child. As soon as this little one becomes familiar with words, the Capricorn love of good manners and behaviour will suffer a few setbacks when faced with little Sagittarius's outspoken openness. These youngsters are great seekers of truth, and saying exactly what they feel when they feel it is second nature to them. They can take, without offence, exactly the same treatment from others so why should people get so upset about it? You'll have to explain, patiently, and with exceptional reasoning, that other people are less secure, and home truths can be hurtful, a concept that may take a wealth of blunders to learn. However, it bodes well for a good relationship that this child puts all his cards on the table. Nothing devious or underhand

about this delightful character. Though little will be necessary in order to support this small Archer's natural self-confidence, Capricorn can go a long way in teaching the more practical essentials that take the risk out of Junior's enthusiastic exploits. Sagittarians tend to rush into things with little preparation and gentle coaxing may get them to understand that a little extra planning and groundwork can get them further in the long run. Don't be too rigid about it though as young Sagittarius loves freedom, so allow just a few well-chosen open doors out of all that Capricorn system, and you'll both stay friends.

...and now the bad news!

It will be difficult for you to resist the temptation to nag this lovable, but sometimes irresponsible, child. Clamping down and imposing severe restrictions will be like keeping a fine stallion in a sheep pen. These little Archers have to roam free and reined in they become rude and surly, kicking out at all authority just for the sake of it. Try to be aware of the differences between you and balance the injection of good common sense with the freedom to make a few blunders in the name of adventure. Many Sagittarians achieve the impossible. If they'd planned and prepared like a Capricornian, they'd have realised it was out of the question and not bothered at all! What a lot we'd miss!

THE AQUARIUS PARENT

The good news!

Your approach to anything and everything is original to say the least. Some would even say eccentric. One thing is certain, you don't follow the crowd just because it's the done thing. The freethinking Aquarian parent is bound to have a few theories on childcare. They won't be traditional and there's a fair chance they'll be flexible. Little Sagittarius, as long as there's plenty of room for movement, will fit in with the wildest avant-garde methods. Fun-loving, freedom-seeking little

Archers will explore happily any new territory with this original inventive parent. Aquarius will love and respect Junior's honest enthusiasm, encouraging the adventurous spirit and sharpening up the youngster's understanding with argument and debates. Good lengthy conversations are the keynote to closeness in this good relationship, though they may have to take place on the move; talking while walking is a Sagittarian favourite. Aquarians enjoy ideas for their own sake whilst Sagittarians see

ideas as leading to action, and this may cause a few setbacks if promises don't get fulfilled. With this little one trust and respect allows no room for double-dealing, and no amount of further promises can make up for that. Small Sagittarians will always tell the truth as they see it even if it's to their disadvantage and this parent has the same high ideals. A close friendly relationship with few clashes. When you're off on a good train of thought or following your latest good cause you can be a little detached in your treatment of those around you. Little Sagittarius will understand this but just for the company, when you're missing, a little pet would enhance your small adventurer's life a hundredfold.

...and now the bad news!

The worst that could happen amongst good friends like you is that you may overlook that your self-reliant youngster, for all her independence, needs plenty of hugs and cuddles. Aquarians can often be just a little bit undemonstrative when the conversation seems to be going so well. Remember that actions speak louder than words for all of the Fire signs and a little squeeze didn't do anybody any harm.

THE PISCES PARENT

The good news!

Piscean parents are gentle, loving, and sensitive to the needs of their children. Rarely strong on authority or sticklers for rigid routine they handle things imaginatively according to the feel of the moment. This will suit little Sagittarius down to the ground. Adventurous, energetic, fun-loving and above all demanding freedom to range far and wide, Junior will find flexibility and masses of stimulation in the fantasy mind of this parent. Both express themselves through feelings, but little

Sagittarius's may be more blunt than this sensitive Piscean's. Honest as the day is long, Junior's road to understanding is questions, questions : 'Why is that lady so fat? Does she eat too much? Is she having a baby? How do you make babies? Why?' No poetic waffling; this one wants a straight answer. The patience of the long-suffering Piscean may be stretched to the limits by the business of trying to soften the impact of such a child's sharp and sometimes unknowingly hurtful arrows. But frank openness and sheer warmth of character

more than compensates for the public blunders that may have to be endured. Junior's love of adventure and sometimes oblivious attitude towards risk may cause the Piscean protectiveness to overwork, but keep it subtle for any hint of 'reins' will send Junior to further extremes, defeating the purpose. You're best when you're sharing activities like story telling (far-distant places and adventures), lots of shared outdoor fun, visits to safari parks (neither approve of zoos with all those cages), pets to care for (the bigger the better for young Sagittarius - big dogs, and at least a try at riding a pony).

...and now the bad news!

Pisceans like Librans like love and harmony to rule so hand to hand fighting is not high on the agenda in a Fishes aquarium. Where love rules where can be the bad news? Well, only that your little one will soon fathom out that you're the softest touch in the zodiac where nearest and dearest are concerned. Little Sagittarius will use this knowledge unscrupulously if you don't draw the line somewhere early on in the relationship. It's tough for you, but being a little firmer now will avoid later becoming the doormat that welcomes your bossy little traveller's homecomings.

ON THE CUSP

Many people whose children are born on the day the sun changes signs are not sure whether they come under one sign or another. Some say one is supposed to be a little bit of each but this is rarely true. Adjoining signs are very different to each other so checking up can make everything clear. The opposite table gives the exact Greenwich Mean Time (GMT) when the sun moves into Sagittarius and when it leaves. Subtract or add the hours indicated below for your nearest big city.

AMSTERDAM	GMT +01.00	MADRID	GMT +01.00
ATHENS	GMT +02.00	MELBOURNE	GMT +10.00
BOMBAY	GMT +05.30	MONTREAL	GMT - 05.00
CAIRO	GMT +02.00	NEW YORK	GMT - 05.00
CALGARY	GMT - 07.00	PARIS	GMT +01.00
CHICAGO	GMT - 06.00	ROME	GMT +01.00
DURBAN	GMT +02.00	S.FRANCISCO	GMT - 08.00
GIBRALTAR	GMT +01.00	SYDNEY	GMT +10.00
HOUSTON	GMT - 06.00	TOKYO	GMT +09.00
LONDON	GMT 00.00	WELLINGTON	GMT +12.00

DATE	ENTERS SAGITTARIUS	GMT	LEAVES SAGITTARIUS	GMT
1984	NOV 22	3.11 AM	DEC 21	4.23 PM
1985	NOV 22	8.51 AM	DEC 21	10.08 PM
1986	NOV 22	2.45 PM	DEC 22	4.03 AM
1987	NOV 22	8.30 PM	DEC 22	9.46 AM
1988	NOV 22	2.12 AM	DEC 21	3.28 PM
1989	NOV 22	8.05 AM	DEC 21	9.22 PM
1990	NOV 22	1.47 PM	DEC 22	3.07 AM
1991	NOV 22	7.36 PM	DEC 22	8.54 AM
1992	NOV 22	1.26 AM	DEC 21	2.43 PM
1993	NOV 22	7.07 AM	DEC 21	8.26 PM
1994	NOV 22	1.06 PM	DEC 22	2.23 AM
1995	NOV 22	7.02 PM	DEC 22	8.17 AM
1996	NOV 22	12.50 AM	DEC 21	2.06 PM
1997	NOV 22	6.48 AM	DEC 21	8.07 PM
1998	NOV 22	12.35 PM	DEC 22	1.57 AM
1999	NOV 22	6.25 PM	DEC 22	7.44 AM
2000	NOV 22	12.20 AM	DEC 21	1.38 PM
2001	NOV 22	6.01 AM	DEC 21	7.22 PM
2002	NOV 22	11.54 AM	DEC 22	1.15 AM
2003	NOV 22	5.44 PM	DEC 22	7.04 AM
2004	NOV 21	11.23 PM	DEC 21	12.42 PM

John Astrop is an astrologer and author, has written and illustrated over two hundred books for children, is a little Scorpio married to a little Cancerian artist, has one little Capricorn psychologist, one little Pisces songwriter, one little Virgo traveller and a little Aries rock guitarist. The cats are little Sagittarians.